ATTENTIVENESS

IVING
THE GOOD LIFE
TOGETHER

ATTENTIVENESS
being present

leader guide

Pamela Dilmore
and Helen R. Neinast

ABINGDON PRESS / Nashville

LIVING THE GOOD LIFE TOGETHER
ATTENTIVENESS: BEING PRESENT
Leader Guide

Copyright © 2006 by Abingdon Press

Scripture quotations in this publication, unless otherwise indicated, are from the New Revised Standard Version of the Bible, copyrighted © 1989 by the Division of Christian Education of the National Council of the Churches of Christ in the United States of America, and are used by permission. Other quotations are taken from the New King James Version, copyrighted © 1982 by Thomas Nelson, Inc. Used by permission. All rights reserved.

Lectio divina steps adapted by permission from *50 Ways to Pray: Practices From Many Traditions and Times*, by Teresa A. Blythe (Abingdon Press, 2006); pages 45–47.

This book is printed on acid-free, elemental chlorine-free paper.

ISBN 0-687-46550-8

06 07 08 09 10 11 12 13 14 15—10 9 8 7 6 5 4 3 2 1
MANUFACTURED IN THE UNITED STATES OF AMERICA

Contents

SESSION PLANS

ADDITIONAL HELPS

Introduction

LIVING THE GOOD LIFE TOGETHER: A STUDY OF CHRISTIAN CHARACTER IN COMMUNITY

Welcome to Living the Good Life Together! This unique and exciting series is designed to help Christians learn about and put into practice various character traits associated with the Christian faith. Some of these character traits are attentiveness, forgiveness, discernment, intimacy, humility, and hospitality.

Christian life invites us to cultivate habits that continually open us and others to God's grace, a grace that reshapes our desires, thoughts, feelings, and actions. The "good life" in Christ is life shaped by God's grace. When we choose to seek this good life together, we are drawn into the disciplined habits of living as friends of God in the community of others.

Jesus' ministry was spent teaching and showing others God's good life, so much so that he invested extraordinary time and energy with his disciples. In John 1:39, Jesus invited would-be followers to "come and see." This is a response that facilitates learning and understanding. Luke 10:37 offers Jesus' instruction to "go and do likewise," the closing words to the parable of the good Samaritan. With these words, Jesus invites listeners to practice what they have learned about compassion and mercy, to go and do what is neighborly.

Learning about and practicing the character traits of the Christian life can be compared to learning how to play the piano. We must learn basics such as the position of our hands, the scales, the foot pedals, rhythm, melody, and reading notes. If we practice, our skill improves. We are able to play music for others as well as for ourselves. And we find joy in the music!

In a similar way, Living the Good Life Together is designed to help us practice being Christian. Each unit is intended to help us *understand* or learn about an aspect of Christian character, then move into the *practice* of what we have learned. Together we will explore and practice ways to *embody* Christian character in community. And we will find joy in the good life!

A billboard or bumper sticker would say it more succinctly: "The Good Life: Get It. Try It. Live It—Together."

ATTENTIVENESS: BEING PRESENT

The Christian character trait featured in this study of Living the Good Life Together is *attentiveness*, or being present to God and to the world. Attentiveness is a basic skill in all human life. As children, we were taught to pay attention so that we might learn. We were taught to stop, look, and listen so that we might be safe. Human activities such as driving, operating machinery or computers, farming and gardening, cooking, playing a musical instrument, caring for children, entertaining guests, reading a book, going to a play, or watching a movie require attentiveness. In fact, it's challenging to think of a human activity other than sleep that does not in some way involve attentiveness.

Since attentiveness is such a basic practice in daily human existence, we may at first wonder why it is considered an important trait of Christian character. Exploring the meanings of the word *attentiveness* offers insight. To attend is to be present, to take care of or look after, to listen to or look at. The word comes from ancient roots that mean to stretch toward something. All these shimmers of meaning radiate from attentiveness. *Christian attentiveness* is the practice of being present, looking, listening, stretching toward God and toward God's ways of life revealed in the world, in Scripture, and through Jesus Christ.

The meanings of the word *attentiveness* contain as a key component an active response of caring for or looking after something or someone. Be still, stop, look, and listen to God; then act according to God's ways. Jesus said, "Come and see" (John 1:39), then "Go and do likewise" (Luke 10:37). Be both hearers and doers of the word (Matthew 7:24; James 1:22-25). Attending to God opens our minds and hearts to God's grace, power, and steadfast love. As we practice attentiveness, we discover God's transforming life. The Scripture says this yet another way: "Seek, and you will find" (Matthew 7:7, NKJV). If we seek God and God's ways through the practice of attentiveness, we will find what we need to live God's way.

Jesus encouraged attentiveness when he spoke about eyes that see (Mark 8:18; Luke 10:23) and ears that hear (Mark 4:9, 23; Luke 8:8; 14:35). The sessions in ATTENTIVENESS: BEING PRESENT rely upon the idea of listening in order to teach about and put into practice several aspects of attentiveness. "Listening to the Right Voices" deals with listening to the voice of God in our noisy world. "Keeping Time" encourages us to make time to listen to God. "Self-Awareness" challenges us to see ourselves as God sees us. "Listening Alone, Listening Together" invites us to pray alone and

9

to pray with others. "Planning the Next Steps Together" facilitates a group planning process for putting into practice what the group has learned about attentiveness. All the sessions help us "stretch toward" God and practice God's ways of attentiveness.

Pay attention. Stop. Look. Listen. Be still. Be present to God. Come and see the practice of attentiveness. Then go and do likewise.

RESOURCE COMPONENTS

The resources and group sessions in this study function together to foster intimacy with Scripture, with God, and with others. The resources include a study & reflection guide for each participant, a DVD for viewing during group sessions, and this leader guide.

Study & Reflection Guide

The study & reflection guide is designed for use by the group participants. Each person in the group should have his or her own copy. This guide contains the core content of the study. It also contains several important features in addition to the core content.

Psalm for Praying

A psalm appears on the first page of each session. The group will use this psalm as a prayer of invocation at the beginning of the session.

Daily Readings

Scripture readings are included for each day of the week between the group sessions. Participants will read and reflect upon these Scriptures and use the space provided to write notes or questions they would like to bring to the group session. You will also do these daily readings.

Reflections

When core content is being introduced, space is provided at the bottom of the page for making notes or recording any thoughts brought to mind by the readings.

Faithful Friends

Each participant will be invited to join with one or two others to practice being a faithful friend over the course of the study and beyond. Spaces are provided at the end of Sessions 2–5 in the study & reflection guide where participants can record thoughts, reflections, insights, prayer concerns, or other matters concerning their faithful friends.

DVD

The video segments on the DVD are designed to supplement the core content presented in the study & reflection guide and to inspire and invite the group into the practice of a particular aspect of Christian character. These segments are 6–10 minutes long and will be viewed during the group sessions, as described in this leader guide.

Leader Guide

The leader guide is designed to help you lead your group with confidence and inspiration. It contains all the information you need in order to help your group plan and carry out the study.

Besides introducing the series and the topic of this particular study, the leader guide also provides detailed session plans. These session plans give you easy-to-follow instructions, including what materials you will need and how to prepare the learning area. The plans also encourage you to set aside a time of preparation before the actual session to prepare yourself spiritually and review your approach to the session.

The leader guide introduces you to the unique "Come and See," "Go and Do" format of the study, including additional helps and examples to use as you implement that format. The leader guide concludes with suggestions for planning a final worship and celebration experience.

STUDY FORMAT

The format of this study series is based on some of Jesus' own words to his followers: "Come and see" (John 1:39), and "Go and do likewise" (Luke 10:37). In each study, the first six sessions are the backbone of the "Come and See" portion. These sessions inspire and teach the group about a particular character trait of the Christian life. The second six sessions are the "Go and Do" portion. For these sessions, the study offers tools to help group members plan how to put into practice what they have learned.

"Come and See"

Session 1: An Introduction to This Study Series

This session is an orientation to the twelve-week study. In the session, group members will learn about the series, the study format, and the particular topic of this study. They will become familiar with the study & reflection guide and learn about the video presentations. They will learn about the term *faithful friends* and about the practice of *lectio divina*.

Sessions 2–5: Topics in Christian Character

These sessions offer information about the aspect of Christian character explored in this particular study. The sessions have a particular format designed to teach participants about that aspect and to foster intimacy with Scripture, with others, and with God.

Session 6: Planning the Next Steps Together

This session facilitates planning for what the group will do together in Sessions 7–12 to practice the Christian character trait they have learned about in the previous sessions. Session 6 in this leader guide, "Planning the Next Steps Together," offers a flexible, step-by-step guide for leading the group through the planning process.

The session builds upon a brainstorming activity that the participants will do before they come together. The participants will write their ideas where prompted in the study & reflection guide before coming to Session 6. Make sure they understand the importance of doing this brainstorming activity ahead of time.

"Go and Do"

Sessions 7–12: Practicing Christian Character

What will the group do?

These "Go and Do" sessions are meant to allow time to live out some of what the group has learned in the "Come and See" portion of the study. The group will put into practice what they planned during Session 6, "Planning the Next Steps Together." The group will also continue the practice of faithful friends throughout this portion of the study.

The group may use these sessions in any number of ways. The idea is to reinforce what they have learned and to deepen their practice of the particular aspect of Christian character. The group might consider planning activities in some of the following categories, which are also given as prompts in the study & reflection guide:

- Lectio divina Scripture passages
- Behavioral changes to make
- Ministry events to consider

- Mission work to conceive and implement
- Speakers to invite
- Field trips, retreats, pilgrimages to take
- Books to read, movies to see

Possibilities for these next sessions can be varied and creative. There are many movies that lend themselves to group study. You could borrow these from your church or a public library or rent them from a video store. Watch these together and discuss. This is a good way to learn more about those in your group as well as about yourself. Is there a book the group could read and discuss together? A series of audio programs? Is there someone in your church or community you'd like to invite to share the group's time together? What about additional Bible study? Would each group member want to bring in something—an article, a story, something found on the Internet—for the group to discuss from week to week?

How often will the group meet?

The group will decide how many times and on what dates they will meet. Your group may want to continue meeting weekly, or they may decide meeting dates based upon the types of activities they choose to do. A retreat, for example, may involve an overnight gathering. A mission experience could involve one day or several days. A book study might involve two or more weekly sessions. The point is to plan activities that the group will do together in order to put into practice what they have learned; then, let the content of what you have planned dictate and shape the frequency and format of your meetings.

The final session, which will also be planned by the group, will be a worship and celebration of what the group has learned and practiced during their time together. It will inspire all who have participated in the study to put into everyday life the practices of Christian character they have explored together. It will offer opportunities to express gratitude and commitment to God. (See ideas for this worship and celebration in the "Additional Helps" section on pages 59–62.)

SESSION ACTIVITIES

During Sessions 1–6, the "Come and See" portion of the study, you will lead your group through a regular sequence of activities described below. These activities are designed to bring the group together, to create an environment for learning, and to help the group use videos, books, Scripture, and group discussion to explore Christian character. Details of how to prepare for and implement these activities, week by week, are spelled out in this leader guide under "Session Plans" (pages 25–57).

During Sessions 7–12, the "Go and Do" portion of the study, your group will be following its own session plans, but you may want to continue some of the activities listed below as a part of those sessions.

Welcome

Greet participants, especially members who are new to the study. Remind them to use nametags, and make them feel welcome.

Psalm and Silence

This is a time to center as a group using the psalms provided in the study & reflection guide. For later sessions, you may choose another Scripture passage or reading.

Look and Listen

The group will view the video segments as described in the session plans. For later sessions, your group can use any other materials they choose, such as books, movies, Scripture passages, and group members' experiences.

Reflect and Respond

This is a time to reflect upon and respond to the content of the particular session. Allow for discussion, dialogue, and questions from everyone in the group.

Lectio Divina

The group will experience the ancient practice of prayerfully reading the Scriptures. The practice is described, step by step, in both the study & reflection guide and the leader guide (see below).

Pray and Practice

This is a time for closing reflections—about the material, about faithful friend experiences, or about prayer concerns. Close this session with prayer in any way your group wishes.

Lectio Divina

Lectio divina, which means "sacred reading," is sometimes also called "praying the Scriptures." It's an ancient process for engaging the Scriptures in order to hear the voice of God. Sessions 1–5 of the study include lectio divina for a particular Scripture related to the topic of the session. Groups may choose to incorporate the practice of lectio divina in later sessions as well.

The lectio divina process contains the following steps:

Step One: *Silencio*

After everyone has turned to the Scripture, be still. Silently turn all your thoughts and desires over to God. Let go of concerns, worries, or agendas. Just *be* for a few minutes.

Step Two: *Lectio*

Read the short passage of Scripture slowly and carefully, either aloud or silently. Reread it. Be alert to any word, phrase, or image that invites you, that puzzles you, that intrigues you. Wait for this word, phrase, or image to come to you; try not to rush it.

Step Three: *Meditatio*

Take the word, phrase, or image from your Scripture passage that comes to you and ruminate over it. Repeat it to yourself. Allow this word, phrase, or image to engage your thoughts, your desires, your memories. Invite anyone who would like to share his or her word, phrase, or image, but don't pressure anyone to speak.

Step Four: *Oratio*

Pray that God transform you through the word, phrase, or image from Scripture. Consider how this word, phrase, or image connects with your life and how God is made known to you in it. This prayer may be either silent or spoken.

Step Five: *Contemplatio*

Rest silently in the presence of God. Move beyond words, phrases, or images. Again, just *be* for a few minutes. Close this time of lectio divina with "Amen."

The steps above are also listed in each session plan. Participants will find these steps in the study & reflection guide on pages 12–13.

FAITHFUL FRIENDS

Each week, pairs or small groups of faithful friends will get together to talk about their experience of practicing the week's discipline. Developing and nurturing faithful friends are important practices that continue throughout the twelve weeks of the study.

The Christian way of life presupposes healthy relationships with God, self, and neighbor in Christ. Learning how to give and to receive the support of a faithful friend is a cornerstone of living the good life together.

The spiritual discipline of faithful friendship may be uncomfortable for some in the group. Some people are quiet and introspective, and the thought of talking about deep, heartfelt issues of Christian faith may feel threatening to them. For this reason, it's important to give a great deal of freedom to the participants in choosing faithful friends and deciding how they wish to support one another during the weeks of the study. The questions listed below can ease faithful friends into conversation in a nonthreatening way.

Faithful friends can stay in touch by e-mail, telephone, or over lunch or coffee. They may think of other ways to stay in touch, such as visiting one another in their homes or enjoying a recreational activity together. In these kinds of activities, encourage participants to take time to talk about the study.

Some faithful friends will appreciate guidance for their conversations together. Encourage them to use the following questions, which are also listed on page 14 in the study & reflection guide.

- How has it gone for you, trying to live the week's practice?
- What's been hard about it?
- What's been easy or comfortable?
- What challenges have there been? What rewards?
- What kinds of things happened this week—at work, at home, in your prayer life—that you want to talk about? Has anything affected your spiritual life and walk?

Faithful friends may meet or communicate as often as they like. The expectation is that they communicate at least once a week. During each session, ask the group as a whole how the practice of faithful friends is going. Ask how they are choosing to communicate. Remind them that faithful friends provide a rewarding way to experience meaningful spiritual growth. Also remind them that they can record any thoughts, reflections, insights, prayer concerns, or other matters concerning their faithful friends in the spaces provided in their study & reflection guide (Sessions 2–5).

Don't ask individual participants to talk about their faithful friends conversations. Doing so may cause embarrassment or unnecessary pressure. As a leader, your comments about the practice of having faithful friends should be supportive and affirming.

If the faithful friends practice doesn't seem to be going well for some of the participants, don't criticize them. Simply suggest a phone call, card, or e-mail saying they are thinking about the faithful friend or praying for them. Every day is a new day that offers many opportunities to support one another. Remind participants to honor confidentiality with their faithful friends, to pray for their faithful friends and for their own role as a faithful friend, to listen deeply to one another, and to demonstrate respect for one another.

How to Organize a Group

Living the Good Life Together is an excellent resource for all people who are looking for meaning in their daily lives, who want to grow in their faith, and who want to practice specific traits of Christian character. Group members may be persons who are not a part of a faith community and yet are seekers on a profound spiritual journey. They may be new Christians or new church members who want to know more about Christian faith. Or they may be people who have been in church a long time but feel a need for spiritual renewal. All such persons desire to engage more deeply with what it means to practice the Christian faith.

In order to start a Living the Good Life Together group, you may want to follow the steps below.

1. Read through the leader guide and the study & reflection guide. View all the video segments on the DVD. Think about

the specific character trait dealt with in the study, the issues it generates, and the Scriptures. Prepare to respond to questions that someone may ask about the study.

2. Develop a list of potential group members. An ideal size for a small group is seven to twelve people. Your list should have about twice your target number (fourteen to twenty-four people). Encourage your local church to purchase a copy of the study & reflection guide for each of the persons on your list. This is an invaluable outreach tool.

3. Decide on a location and time for your group.

4. Identify someone who is willing to go with you to visit the persons on your list. Make it your goal to become acquainted with each person you visit. Tell them about Living the Good Life Together. Give them a copy of the study & reflection guide. Even if they choose not to attend the group at this time, they will have an opportunity to study the book on their own. Tell each person the initial meeting time, location, and how many weeks the group will meet. Invite them to become a part of the group. Thank them for their time.

5. Publicize the study through as many channels as are available. Announce it during worship. Print notices in the church newsletter and bulletin and on the church website if you have one. Use free public-event notices in community newspapers. Create flyers for mailing and posting in public places.

6. A few days before the sessions begin, give a friendly phone call or send an e-mail to thank all persons you visited for their consideration and interest. Remind them of the time and location of the first meeting.

HOW TO LEAD A GROUP

The role of the leader is to use the resources and facilitate the group sessions in order to foster intimacy with Scripture, with God, and with others. So what does a leader do?

A Leader Prepares

This leader guide contains specific instructions for planning and implementing the study. Generally speaking, however, a leader has some basic preparation responsibilities. They are:

Pray

Ask for God's guidance as you prepare to lead the session.

Read

Review the session materials and its Scriptures ahead of time. Jot down questions or insights that occur during the reading.

Think About Group Participants

Who are they? What life issues or questions might they have about the theme? About the Scriptures?

Prepare the Learning Area

Gather any needed supplies, such as large sheets of paper, markers, paper and pencils, Bibles, hymn books, audiovisual equipment, masking tape, a Bible dictionary, or Bible commentaries. If you are meeting in a classroom setting, arrange the chairs in a semicircle so that everyone can easily see the video segments that will be shown during the session. Make sure everyone will have a place to sit.

Pray for the Group Participants

Before the participants arrive, pray for each one. Ask for God's blessing on your session. Offer thanks to God for the opportunity to lead the session.

A Leader Creates a Welcoming Atmosphere

Hospitality is a spiritual discipline. A leader helps to create an environment that makes others feel welcome and helps every participant experience the freedom to ask questions and to state opinions. Such an atmosphere is based upon mutual respect.

Greet Participants as They Arrive

Say out loud the name of each participant. If the class is meeting for the first time, use nametags.

Listen

As group discussion unfolds, affirm the comments and ideas of participants. Avoid the temptation to dominate conversation or "correct" the ideas of participants.

Affirm

Thank people for telling about what they think or feel. Acknowledge their contributions to discussion in positive ways, even if you disagree with their ideas.

A Leader Facilitates Discussion

Ask Questions

Use the questions suggested in the session plans or other questions that occur to you as you prepare for the session. Encourage others to ask questions.

Invite Silent Participants to Contribute Ideas

If someone in the group is quiet, you might say something like, "I'm interested in what you're thinking." If participants seem hesitant or shy, don't pressure them to speak. However, do communicate your interest.

Gently Redirect Discussion When Someone in the Group Dominates

You can do this in several ways. Remind the group as a whole that everyone's ideas are important. Invite them to respect one another and to allow others the opportunity to express their ideas. You may establish a group covenant that clarifies such mutual respect. Use structured methods such as going around the circle to allow everyone a chance to speak. Only as a last resort, speak to the person who dominates conversation after the group meeting.

Session Plans

1. An Introduction to This Study Series

Prepare for the Session

Let your preparation for the session be a time to pay attention to God and to the needs of group members as well as a time to review the content of the session. Find a quiet and comfortable place where you will not be interrupted. Have the DVD, a Bible, and the study & reflection guide available in addition to this leader guide. Have paper and pen available to jot down notes or insights. You may wish to keep these notes in a personal journal during this study.

Pray, asking for God's guidance as you prepare for the session. Read Psalm 84:1-4. Take a moment to reflect upon how this psalm speaks to you.

Review the information about Living the Good Life Together in the introduction to the leader guide to make sure you understand the process for the sessions in the series. Anticipate questions group members might have about the program. Write down any notes and questions you have.

View the video segments "Series Overview" and "*Come and See: Preview.*" Write notes and questions suggested by the video segments. If you have time, view all the video segments in the study in order to have a more complete overview.

Read the introduction to the series in the study & reflection guide. Write notes and questions suggested by the material.

Review the information about lectio divina in the introduction to the leader guide (pages 16–17). Read Matthew 6:25-34 using this process. Write notes or questions that emerge from your reading.

Review the information about faithful friends in the introduction to the leader guide and in the instructions below. Make sure you understand the purpose and process for this practice. Consider ways to support and encourage the process for the group members.

Review the steps in "Lead the Session." Pray, offering gratitude to God for insights, ideas, and guidance for the session. Give thanks for the group members and for what you will experience together.

Gather Materials and Set Up the Learning Area

- Bibles
- DVD, DVD player, and TV
- Leader guide
- Study & reflection guides, one for each participant
- Nametags and markers or pens
- Chairs in a semicircle for viewing the video

Lead the Session

Welcome (3 minutes)

Greet participants as they arrive. Invite them to make a nametag and to find a place to sit where they can comfortably view the video.

Psalm and Silence (3 minutes)

A psalm for praying appears on the first page of each session of the study & reflection guide. This session is "An Introduction to This Study Series," so participants will not yet have the printed material in front of them for the psalm. Read Psalm 84:1-4 as a prayer of invocation. Follow the praying of the psalm with at least a minute of silence.

Look and Listen (8 minutes)

Introduce the first video segment as follows: "This video presentation offers an overview of our study of Living the Good Life Together. It will invite us to consider the Christian character trait of attentiveness." Then view the video segment "Series Overview."

Reflect and Respond (5 minutes)

Following the video, lead the group in discussing the following questions:

- Whom did you recognize in the photographs at the beginning of the video? What thoughts or feelings did these images evoke for you?
- Learning to play the piano illustrates the need to practice in order to learn a skill. What do you remember about learning a new skill? How does this connect to learning to live as a Christian?

27

Overview of Living the Good Life Together (8 minutes)

Tell About the Study Format

Tell the group members about how Living the Good Life Together will work. The total time for the study is twelve weeks. The structure of the study is based upon Jesus' words to the disciples. The first six sessions, "Come and See," will focus on learning and understanding.

Read aloud John 1:38-39. Tell the group that the "Come and See" part of the study is based upon this Scripture.

The second six sessions, "Go and Do," will focus on application or practice. Read aloud Luke 10:36-37, the end of the parable of the good Samaritan. Tell the group that the "Go and Do" part of the study is based upon this Scripture.

Session 6 of the "Come and See" part will be a group planning time for Sessions 7–12. The group will make plans for "Go and Do" based upon what they have learned in "Come and See." Session 12 will conclude with a worship and celebration for the study on attentiveness.

Tell About the Study & Reflection Guide

Give each participant a study & reflection guide. Tell them to turn to pages 11–12. Together, look at the section describing the study & reflection guide. Read aloud the paragraphs entitled "Psalm for Praying," "Daily Readings," and "Reflections."

Tell About the Video Segments

Tell participants that the group sessions will include a brief video segment designed to inspire and to invite reflection and discussion about attentiveness. The video segments supplement and enhance the core content presented in the study & reflection guide.

Faithful Friends (5 minutes)

Ask the group to look at the section on faithful friends on pages 13–14 of the study & reflection guide. You may say something like the following:

- Pairs or small groups of faithful friends will get together during the week to talk about their experiences with the study. This might be over lunch or coffee, during a walk, or by phone or e-mail.
- Use the following questions to help start your conversation:
  - ✓ How has it gone for you, trying to live the week's practice?
  - ✓ What's been hard about it?
  - ✓ What's been easy or comfortable?
  - ✓ What challenges have there been? What rewards?
  - ✓ What kinds of things happened this week—at work, at home, in your prayer life—that you want to talk about? Has anything affected your spiritual life and walk?
- Ask group members to find a partner or partners. You may ask people to pair up on their own, or you may have people number off to get into pairs. If the group has an odd number of people, ask one group to form as three. Be sure to include yourself in this process of forming faithful friends. Tell the group there will be suggestions at the end of today's session for what they might do this week as faithful friends.

Overview of ATTENTIVENESS: BEING PRESENT *(5 minutes)*

Ask participants to look on pages 14–16 in the study & reflection guide at the section called "Attentiveness: Being Present." Share in your own words the information from the introduction to this leader guide under "Attentiveness: Being Present" (pages 8–10). Emphasize the following points from this material:

- Attentiveness is a basic human practice necessary for daily living.

- To attend is to be present, to take care of or look after, to listen to or look at. The word comes from ancient roots that mean to stretch toward something.
- *Christian attentiveness* is the practice of being present, looking, listening, stretching toward God and toward God's ways of life revealed in the world, in Scripture, and through Jesus Christ.
- The meaning of the word *attentiveness* contains as a key component an active response of caring for or looking after something or someone.
- Jesus encouraged attentiveness when he spoke about eyes that see (Mark 8:18; Luke 10:23) and ears that hear (Mark 4:9, 23; Luke 8:8; 14:35).
- This study relies upon the idea of listening in order to teach about and put into practice several aspects of attentiveness. Session 2, "Listening to the Right Voices," deals with listening to the voice of God in our noisy world. Session 3, "Keeping Time," encourages us to make time to listen to God. Session 4, "Self-Awareness," challenges us to see ourselves as God sees us. Session 5, "Listening Alone, Listening Together," invites us to pray alone and to pray with others. Session 6, "Planning the Next Steps Together," facilitates group planning for putting into practice what the group has learned about attentiveness.
- In this study, we are invited to: Pay attention. Stop. Look. Listen. Be still. Be present to God. Come and see the Christian practice of attentiveness. Then go and do likewise.

Lectio Divina (10 minutes)

For this introductory session, the group will not have read any Bible passages or chapter content. Have someone read aloud Matthew 6:25-34, the story of the lilies of the field. Ask what this Scripture means in light of the theme of attentiveness.

Tell the group that they will use the ancient practice of lectio divina to prayerfully engage Matthew 6:25-34. As a group, use the lectio divina approach outlined as follows to pray this Scripture.

Step One: *Silencio*

After everyone has turned to the Scripture, be still. Silently turn all your thoughts and desires over to God. Let go of concerns, worries, or agendas. Just *be* for a few minutes.

Step Two: *Lectio*

Read the short passage of Scripture slowly and carefully, either aloud or silently. Reread it. Be alert to any word, phrase, or image that invites you, that puzzles you, that intrigues you. Wait for this word, phrase, or image to come to you; try not to rush it.

Step Three: *Meditatio*

Take the word, phrase, or image from your Scripture passage that comes to you and ruminate over it. Repeat it to yourself. Allow this word, phrase, or image to engage your thoughts, your desires, your memories. Invite anyone who would like to share his or her word, phrase, or image, but don't pressure anyone to speak.

Step Four: *Oratio*

Pray that God transform you through the word, phrase, or image from Scripture. Consider how this word, phrase, or image connects with your life and how God is made known to you in it. This prayer may be either silent or spoken.

Step Five: *Contemplatio*

Rest silently in the presence of God. Move beyond words, phrases, or images. Again, just *be* for a few minutes. Close this time of lectio divina with "Amen."

Look and Listen (6 minutes)

Introduce the second video segment as follows: "This video presentation offers a preview of our study of attentiveness. It will invite us to consider the spiritual discipline of attentiveness in the

31

context of our often-chaotic culture." Then view the video segment *"Come and See:* Preview."

Pray and Practice (5 minutes)

This Week's Practice

Encourage group members to do the following:

- Contact their faithful friend this week for coffee, lunch, a walk, or a phone conversation, and talk with that friend about his or her experience of practicing attentiveness this week. Remind them to use the list of questions in the faithful friends section of Session 1, "An Introduction to This Study Series," in the study & reflection guide (pages 13–14).
- Do the daily readings listed in Session 2, "Listening to the Right Voices," in the study & reflection guide (pages 18–19).
- In the study & reflection guide, review Session 1, "An Introduction to This Study Series." Then read Session 2, "Listening to the Right Voices" (pages 20–25), and write notes or questions for discussion in the reflections space.

Closing Prayer

- Share prayer concerns.
- Invite participants to pray for their faithful friend and for the group this week.
- Imagine and discuss possible steps that group members might take this week to put into practice the week's learnings.

Close with a prayer asking God to support each participant. Pray that group members will sense God's support and the encouragement of the group as they seek ways to practice attentiveness during the weeks ahead.

2. LISTENING TO THE RIGHT VOICES

Prepare for the Session

Let your preparation for the session be a time to pay attention to God and to the needs of group members as well as a time to review the content of the session. Find a quiet and comfortable place where you will not be interrupted. Have the DVD, a Bible, and the study & reflection guide available in addition to this leader guide. Have paper and pen available to jot down notes or insights.

Pray, asking God's guidance as you prepare for the session. Read Psalm 42:1-6a prayerfully.

View the video segment "Listening to the Right Voices." Write notes and questions suggested by the video.

Read Session 2, "Listening to the Right Voices," in the study & reflection guide, as well as the Scriptures mentioned in the daily readings and text. Write notes and questions suggested by the material.

Review the description of lectio divina in the introduction to this leader guide (pages 16–17). Read Romans 12:1-2 using this process. Write notes or questions that emerge from your reading.

Review the steps in "Lead the Session." Pray, offering gratitude to God for insights, ideas, and guidance during the session. Offer gratitude for the group members and for what you will experience together.

Gather Materials and Set Up the Learning Area

- Bibles
- DVD, DVD player, and TV
- Leader guide
- Study & reflection guide, one for each participant (participants may bring their own copies)
- Nametags and markers or pens
- Chairs in a semicircle for viewing the video

Lead the Session

Welcome (5 minutes)

Greet participants as they arrive. Invite them to take a name-tag and to find a place to sit where they can comfortably view the video.

Psalm and Silence (3 minutes)

Read Psalm 42:1-6a as a prayer of invocation. Follow the praying of the psalm with at least a minute of silence.

Look and Listen (10 minutes)

Introduce the video segment as follows: "This video presentation invites us to hear God speaking in a way that changes how we think and how we live." Then view the video segment "Listening to the Right Voices."

Reflect and Respond (25 minutes)

Following the video segment, lead the group in discussing these questions:

- Which part of this video spoke most strongly to you? Why?
- What distractions keep you from listening to the voice of God in the way you would like?

Invite participants to recall the daily readings in the Bible done in preparation for the group meeting. Ask:

- What did the Scriptures say to you about attentiveness?
- What did the Scriptures say to you about "listening to the right voices"?

Invite participants to recall their reading this week in Session 2 of the study & reflection guide. Ask:

- What thoughts or questions did you write in the spaces for reflection?
- How do you respond to the statement that more choice often means less happiness? Do you agree or disagree with this statement? Explain.
- Whose voice do we follow? The voice of the world we are *born* into ("Look out for number one. Do whatever feels right to you.") or the voice of the world we are *baptized* into ("Follow the Spirit's guiding. Put God first in your life.")? When in your life was it difficult to distinguish between the two? What tests can you use to help discern that a voice is from God?
- Consider and discuss this statement: "Often we discover that in reading Scripture, Scripture is actually reading us."

Lectio Divina (10 minutes)

As a group, use the approach outlined as follows to pray this Scripture: Romans 12:1-2.

Step One: *Silencio*

After everyone has turned to the Scripture, be still. Silently turn all your thoughts and desires over to God. Let go of concerns, worries, or agendas. Just *be* for a few minutes.

Step Two: *Lectio*

Read the short passage of Scripture slowly and carefully, either aloud or silently. Reread it. Be alert to any word, phrase, or image that invites you, that puzzles you, that intrigues you. Wait for this word, phrase, or image to come to you; try not to rush it.

Step Three: *Meditatio*

Take the word, phrase, or image from your Scripture passage that comes to you and ruminate over it. Repeat it to yourself. Allow this word, phrase, or image to engage your thoughts, your desires, your memories. Invite anyone who would like to share his or her word, phrase, or image, but don't pressure anyone to speak.

Step Four: *Oratio*

Pray that God transform you through the word, phrase, or image from Scripture. Consider how this word, phrase, or image connects with your life and how God is made known to you in it. This prayer may be either silent or spoken.

Step Five: *Contemplatio*

Rest silently in the presence of God. Move beyond words, phrases, or images. Again, just *be* for a few minutes. Close this time of lectio divina with "Amen."

Pray and Practice (5 minutes)

This Week's Practice

Encourage group members to do the following:

- Contact their faithful friend this week and talk with that friend about his or her experience of listening to God's voice. Remind them to use the list of questions in the faithful friends section of Session 1, "An Introduction to This Study Series," in the study & reflection guide (pages 13–14).
- Do the daily readings listed in Session 3, "Keeping Time," in the study & reflection guide (pages 28–29).
- Read Session 3, "Keeping Time," in the study & reflection guide (pages 30–35). Write notes or questions for reflection or discussion in the reflections space.

Closing Prayer

- Share prayer concerns.
- Invite participants to pray for their faithful friend and for the group this week.
- Imagine and discuss possible steps that group members might take to put into practice the week's learnings about listening to the right voices.

Close with a prayer asking God to support each participant. Pray that group members will sense God's support and the encouragement of the group as they seek ways to make time to listen to God's voice in spite of the distractions of daily life.

3. KEEPING TIME

Prepare for the Session

Let your preparation for the session be a time to pay attention to God and to the needs of group members as well as a time to review the content of the session. Find a quiet and comfortable place where you will not be interrupted. Have the DVD, a Bible, and the study & reflection guide available in addition to this leader guide. Have paper and pen available to jot down notes or insights.

Pray, asking God's guidance as you prepare for the session. Read Psalm 90:1-2, 14-17 prayerfully.

View the video segment "Keeping Time." Write notes and questions suggested by the video.

Read Session 3, "Keeping Time," in the study & reflection guide and the Scriptures mentioned in the daily readings and text. Write notes and questions suggested by the material.

Review the description of lectio divina in the introduction to this leader guide (pages 16–17). Read Luke 10:38-42 using this process. Write notes or questions that emerge from your reading.

Review the steps in "Lead the Session." Pray, offering gratitude to God for insights, ideas, and guidance for the session. Offer gratitude for the group members and for what you will experience together.

Gather Materials and Set Up the Learning Area

- Bibles
- DVD, DVD player, and TV
- Leader guide
- Study & reflection guide, one for each participant (participants may bring their own copies)
- Nametags and markers or pens
- Chairs in a semicircle for viewing the video

Lead the Session

Welcome (5 minutes)

Greet participants as they arrive. Invite them to take a name-tag and to find a place to sit where they can comfortably view the video.

Psalm and Silence (3 minutes)

Read Psalm 90:1-2, 14-17 as a prayer of invocation. Follow the praying of the psalm with at least a minute of silence.

Look and Listen (10 minutes)

Introduce the video segment as follows: "This video presentation offers reflections on our cluttered lives and on the importance of making time for God." Then view the video segment "Keeping Time."

Reflect and Respond (25 minutes)

Following the video, lead the group in discussing these questions:

- What thoughts or feelings emerged for you as you watched the video segment?
- What clutters your calendar?
- What insights did you gain from viewing the video that would help you sort through your calendar clutter?

Invite participants to recall the daily readings in the Bible that were done in preparation for the group meeting. Ask:

- What did the Scriptures say to you about attentiveness?
- How did the Scriptures speak to you about keeping time?

Invite participants to recall the session material they read for the this week. Ask:

- What thoughts or questions did you write in the reflection spaces?
- How do we choose between what seems urgent and what really is important?
- What does "sabbath-keeping" mean to you? How might this practice help your busyness? What insights did the session material offer to you about the holiness of the sabbath? How does Jesus' view of the sabbath offer help?
- What insights did you gain from the information about *chronos* time and *kairos* time?

Lectio Divina (10 minutes)

As a group, use the approach outlined as follows to pray this Scripture: Luke 10:38-42.

Step One: *Silencio*

After everyone has turned to the Scripture, be still. Silently turn all your thoughts and desires over to God. Let go of concerns, worries, or agendas. Just *be* for a few minutes.

Step Two: *Lectio*

Read the short passage of Scripture slowly and carefully, either aloud or silently. Reread it. Be alert to any word, phrase, or image that invites you, that puzzles you, that intrigues you. Wait for this word, phrase, or image to come to you; try not to rush it.

Step Three: *Meditatio*

Take the word, phrase, or image from your Scripture passage that comes to you and ruminate over it. Repeat it to yourself. Allow this word, phrase, or image to engage your thoughts, your desires, your memories. Invite anyone who would like to share his or her word, phrase, or image, but don't pressure anyone to speak.

Step Four: *Oratio*

Pray that God transform you through the word, phrase, or image from Scripture. Consider how this word, phrase, or image connects with your life and how God is made known to you in it. This prayer may be either silent or spoken.

Step Five: *Contemplatio*

Rest silently in the presence of God. Move beyond words, phrases, or images. Again, just *be* for a few minutes. Close this time of lectio divina with "Amen."

Pray and Practice (5 minutes)

This week's practice

Encourage group members to do the following:

- Contact their faithful friend this week. Ask them to talk with their faithful friend about calendar clutter, busyness, and the sabbath. Remind them to use the list of questions in the faithful friends section of Session 1, "An Introduction to This Study Series," in the study & reflection guide (pages 13–14).
- Do the daily readings listed in Session 4, "Self-Awareness," in the study & reflection guide (pages 38–39).
- Read Session 4, "Self-Awareness," in the study & reflection guide (pages 40–45). Write notes or questions for reflection or discussion in the reflections space.

Closing Prayer

- Share prayer concerns.
- Invite participants to pray for their faithful friend and for the group this week.

• Imagine and discuss possible steps that group members might take to put into practice the week's learnings about keeping time.

Close with a prayer asking God to support each participant. Pray that group members will gain a sense of how to determine what is really important as they deal with distractions and busyness in their lives.

4. SELF-AWARENESS

Prepare for the Session

Let your preparation for the session be a time to pay attention to God and to the needs of group members as well as a time to review the content of the session. Find a quiet and comfortable place where you will not be interrupted. Have the DVD, a Bible, and the study & reflection guide available in addition to this leader guide. Have paper and pen available to jot down notes or insights.

Pray, asking God's guidance as you prepare for the session. Read Psalm 139:1-3, 23-24 prayerfully.

View the video segment "Self-Awareness." Write notes and questions suggested by the video.

Read Session 4, "Self-Awareness," in the study & reflection guide, as well as the Scriptures mentioned in the daily readings and text. Write notes and questions suggested by the material.

Review the description of lectio divina in the introduction to this leader guide (pages 16–17). Read Matthew 17:1-8 using this process. Write notes or questions that emerge from your reading.

Review the steps in "Lead the Session." Pray, offering gratitude to God for insights, ideas, and guidance for the session. Offer gratitude for the group members and for what you will experience together.

Gather Materials and Set Up the Learning Area

- Bibles
- DVD, DVD player, and TV
- Leader guide
- Study & reflection guide, one for each participant (participants may bring their own copies)
- Nametags and markers or pens
- Chairs in a semicircle for viewing the video

Lead the Session

Welcome (5 minutes)

Greet participants as they arrive. Invite them to take a name-tag and to find a place to sit where they can comfortably view the video.

Psalm and Silence (3 minutes)

Read Psalm 139:1-3, 23-24 as a prayer of invocation. Follow the praying of the psalm with at least a minute of silence.

Look and Listen (10 minutes)

Introduce the video segment as follows: "This video presentation offers reflections that help us consider ourselves as God sees us." Then view the video segment "Self-Awareness."

Reflect and Respond (25 minutes)

Following the video, lead the group in discussing these questions:

- What thoughts or feelings emerged for you as you watched the video segment?
- How did the video help you to think about your own identity?
- When have you wanted to avoid listening to what God desires for you? Why?
- In your life, which voice defines who you understand yourself to be: society's voice or God's voice? What would happen in your life if you listened to God's voice more often?

Invite the participants to recall the daily readings in the Bible done in preparation for the group meeting. Ask:

- What did the Scriptures say to you about attentiveness?
- How did the Scriptures speak to you about self-awareness?

Invite participants to recall the session material they read for this week. Ask:

- What thoughts or questions did you write in the reflection spaces?
- How do you understand the statement "Too often the church has looked for God in places where the world tells us God should be"?
- What thoughts in the Bonhoeffer poem "Who Am I?" (pages 43–44) speak most to you? Why?
- What would it take for us to "see ourselves rightly"? How do you think God sees you? How does God's vision of you compare or contrast with your self-image?

Lectio Divina (10 minutes)

As a group, use the approach outlined as follows to pray this Scripture: Matthew 17:1-8.

Step One: *Silencio*

After everyone has turned to the Scripture, be still. Silently turn all your thoughts and desires over to God. Let go of concerns, worries, or agendas. Just *be* for a few minutes.

Step Two: *Lectio*

Read the short passage of Scripture slowly and carefully, either aloud or silently. Reread it. Be alert to any word, phrase, or image that invites you, that puzzles you, that intrigues you. Wait for this word, phrase, or image to come to you; try not to rush it.

Step Three: *Meditatio*

Take the word, phrase, or image from your Scripture passage that comes to you and ruminate over it. Repeat it to yourself. Allow this word, phrase, or image to engage your thoughts, your desires, your memories. Invite anyone who would like to share his or her word, phrase, or image, but don't pressure anyone to speak.

Step Four: *Oratio*

Pray that God transform you through the word, phrase, or image from Scripture. Consider how this word, phrase, or image connects with your life and how God is made known to you in it. This prayer may be either silent or spoken.

Step Five: *Contemplatio*

Rest silently in the presence of God. Move beyond words, phrases, or images. Again, just *be* for a few minutes. Close this time of lectio divina with "Amen."

Pray and Practice (5 minutes)

This week's practice

Encourage group members to do the following:

- Contact their faithful friend this week. Ask them to talk with that friend about self-awareness in light of God's awareness of who we are. Remind them to use the list of questions in the faithful friends section of Session 1, "An Introduction to This Study Series," in the study & reflection guide (pages 13–14).
- Do the daily readings listed in Session 5, "Listening Alone, Listening Together," in the study & reflection guide (pages 48–49).
- Read Session 5, "Listening Alone, Listening Together," in the study & reflection guide (pages 50–55). Write notes or questions for reflection or discussion in the reflections space.

46

- Read Session 5, "Listening Alone, Listening Together," in the study & reflection guide (pages 50–55). Write notes or questions for reflection or discussion in the reflections space.

Closing Prayer

- Share prayer concerns.
- Invite participants to pray for their faithful friend and for the group this week.
- Imagine and discuss possible steps that group members might take to put into practice what they learned this week about self-awareness.

Close with a prayer asking God to support each participant. Pray that each participant will be encouraged to spend time listening to God's desires for their life and that they will understand themselves as being deeply beloved in God's eyes.

5. LISTENING ALONE, LISTENING TOGETHER

Prepare for the Session

Let your preparation for the session be a time to pay attention to God and to the needs of group members as well as a time to review the content of the session. Find a quiet and comfortable place where you will not be interrupted. Have the DVD, a Bible, and the study & reflection guide available in addition to this leader guide. Have paper and pen available to jot down notes or insights.

Pray, asking God's guidance as you prepare for the session. Read Psalm 46:1-3, 10-11 prayerfully.

View the video segment "Listening Alone, Listening Together." Write notes and questions suggested by the video.

Read Session 5, "Listening Alone, Listening Together," in the study & reflection guide, as well as the Scriptures mentioned in the daily readings and text. Write notes and questions suggested by the material.

Review the description of lectio divina in the introduction to this leader guide (pages 16–17). Read Luke 11:1-4 using this process. Write notes or questions that emerge from your reading.

Review the steps in "Lead the Session." Pray, offering gratitude to God for insights, ideas, and guidance for the session. Offer gratitude for the group members and for what you will experience together.

Gather Materials and Set Up the Learning Area

- Bibles
- DVD, DVD player, and TV
- Leader guide
- Study & reflection guide, one for each participant (participants may bring their own copies)
- Nametags and markers or pens
- Chairs in a semicircle for viewing the video

48

Lead the Session

Welcome (5 minutes)

Greet participants as they arrive. Invite them to take a name-tag and to find a place to sit where they can comfortably view the video.

Psalm and Silence (3 minutes)

Read Psalm 46:1-3, 10-11 as a prayer of invocation. Follow the praying of the psalm with at least a minute of silence.

Look and Listen (10 minutes)

Introduce the video segment as follows: "This video presentation offers ideas about praying alone and praying as a group." Then view the video segment "Listening Alone, Listening Together."

Reflect and Respond (25 minutes)

Following the video, lead the group in discussing these questions:

- What thoughts or feelings emerged for you as you watched the video segment?
- How did the video segment help you to think about praying alone? About praying together?

Invite participants to recall the daily readings in the Bible that were done in preparation for the group meeting. Ask:

- What did the Scriptures say to you about attentiveness?
- How did the Scriptures speak to you about listening to God alone and listening to God together?

Invite participants to recall the session material they read for this week. Ask:

- What thoughts or questions did you write in the reflection spaces?
- How does the experience you have had with lectio divina over the past few weeks compare or contrast with what is described in the session material? How does it compare or contrast with the experience featured in the video segment?
- How does your experience as a faithful friend compare or contrast with what is described in the session material?
- How do you understand prayer? What benefits do you see in praying alone? In praying together?

Lectio Divina (10 minutes)

As a group, use the approach outlined as follows to pray this Scripture: Luke 11:1-4.

Step One: *Silencio*

After everyone has turned to the Scripture, be still. Silently turn all your thoughts and desires over to God. Let go of concerns, worries, or agendas. Just *be* for a few minutes.

Step Two: *Lectio*

Read the short passage of Scripture slowly and carefully, either aloud or silently. Reread it. Be alert to any word, phrase, or image that invites you, that puzzles you, that intrigues you. Wait for this word, phrase, or image to come to you; try not to rush it.

Step Three: *Meditatio*

Take the word, phrase, or image from your Scripture passage that comes to you and ruminate over it. Repeat it to yourself. Allow this word, phrase, or image to engage your thoughts, your desires, your memories. Invite anyone who would like to share his or her word, phrase, or image, but don't pressure anyone to speak.

Step Four: *Oratio*

Pray that God transform you through the word, phrase, or image from Scripture. Consider how this word, phrase, or image connects with your life and how God is made known to you in it. This prayer may be either silent or spoken.

Step Five: *Contemplatio*

Rest silently in the presence of God. Move beyond words, phrases, or images. Again, just *be* for a few minutes. Close this time of lectio divina with "Amen."

Pray and Practice (5 minutes)

This Week's Practice

Encourage group members to do the following:

• Contact their faithful friend this week. Ask them to talk with that friend about praying alone and praying together, about lectio divina, and about faithful friends. Remind them to use the list of questions in the faithful friends section of Session 1, "An Introduction to This Study Series," in the study & reflection guide (pages 13–14).

• Read Session 6, "Planning the Next Steps Together," in the study & reflection guide (pages 58–59). Write ideas in the boxes provided (pages 60–61). Remind the group that Session 6 is a planning session for what the group will do together for the second phase of the study, "Go and Do." The success of Session 6 will depend upon each member of the group brainstorming ideas during the coming week in preparation for the group meeting.

- Continue the practice of lectio divina on their own and with others.

Closing Prayer

- Share prayer concerns.
- Invite participants to pray for their faithful friend and for the group this week.
- Imagine and discuss possible steps that group members might take to put into practice the week's learnings about listening alone and listening together.

Close with a prayer asking God to support each participant. Pray that group members will be encouraged to pray daily, alone and with other people.

6. PLANNING THE NEXT STEPS TOGETHER

Prepare for the Session

Let your preparation for the session be a time to pay attention to God and to the needs of group members as well as a time to review the content of the session. Find a quiet and comfortable place where you will not be interrupted. Have the DVD, a Bible, and the study & reflection guide available in addition to this leader guide. Have paper and pen available to jot down notes or insights.

Pray, asking God's guidance as you prepare for the session. Read Psalm 86:11-12 prayerfully.

Review the information about "Go and Do" in the introduction to this leader guide (pages 13–15) to make sure you understand the planning process for the remaining six sessions. Anticipate questions the group members might have about the program. Write notes and questions you have.

Read Session 6, "Planning the Next Steps Together," in the study & reflection guide (pages 58–59). Write notes and questions suggested by the material. Brainstorm ideas for what you might do as a group over the next six weeks using the idea prompts at the end of the study & reflection guide (pages 60–61).

View the video segment "*Go and Do:* Review and a Challenge." Write notes and questions suggested by the video.

Review the steps in "Lead the Session." Pray, offering gratitude to God for insights, ideas, and guidance for the session. Offer gratitude for the group members and for what you will experience together.

Gather Materials and Set Up the Learning Area

- Bibles
- DVD, DVD player, and TV
- Leader guide
- Study & reflection guide, one for each participant (participants may bring their own copies)

- Nametags and markers or pens
- Whiteboard and markers, chalkboard and chalk, or a large sheet of paper and markers
- Masking tape
- Pens or pencils
- Chairs arranged in a semicircle for viewing the video

Lead the Session

Welcome (3 minutes)

Greet participants as they arrive. Invite them to find a place to sit where they can comfortably view the video.

Psalm and Silence (5 minutes)

Read Psalm 86:11-12 as a prayer of invocation. Follow the praying of the psalm with at least a minute of silence.

Look and Listen (8 minutes)

Introduce the video segment as follows: "This video presentation offers a review of what we have studied in the 'Come and See' portion of our study. It also offers a challenge to practice what we have learned." View the video segment "*Go and Do: Review and a Challenge.*"

Reflect and Respond (5 minutes)

Ask the following questions to stimulate discussion:

- How do you understand the challenge presented in the video segment?
- What learnings did you write about in your study & reflection guide as you prepared for today's session? What connections

do you see between your learnings and the review of highlights presented in the video segment?

Plan Together (30 minutes)

Say something like the following: "During this session, we will plan together how we as a group will put into practice what we have learned about attentiveness. Our plan should reinforce what we have learned, set up future meetings so that we can practice what we have learned and learn more through our practice, and deepen our practice of being a faithful friend. We can use our next six weeks in many ways. We are the ones who will decide what we will do and when we will meet."

Explore Together

Discuss which aspects of the study of attentiveness your group wants to explore in the weeks ahead: listening to the right voices, keeping time, self-awareness, or listening alone and listening together. It's not necessary to choose one session only, but it may be helpful to learn which sessions had the most meaning for the group so that they might explore those topics more in-depth. Use this discussion as a way of working through a list of ideas.

List and Select Ideas

Invite the group to say what ideas they brainstormed and wrote down in the boxes provided in Session 6 of their study & reflection guide (pages 60–61). Create a master list of their suggestions on a large sheet of paper, a chalkboard, or a whiteboard using the same idea prompts found in the boxes in the study & reflection guide. After you have listed all the group's ideas, give participants a marker and invite them to make a checkmark beside the five they like best. Ask them to consider the ideas in light of their discussion on the most meaningful topics. List the ones that receive the most checkmarks. If you have more than five in the list, continue the process until it's reduced to five ideas. You will use this list as a source for scheduling the next six weeks. *Be sure to include a closing worship and celebration for the final session.* (See ideas for this concluding worship and celebration in the "Additional Helps" section on page 62 in this leader guide.)

Create a Schedule

Decide how many times and on what dates you will meet over the next six weeks. Some of your ideas may require meeting weekly. Other ideas may require another schedule. Meeting dates will be based upon the types of activities you choose to do. For example, a retreat may involve an overnight gathering. A mission experience could involve one day or several days. A book study might involve two or more weekly sessions. The point is to plan activities that you will do together in order to put into practice what you have learned. The schedule will emerge from the activities that you choose. Whatever your schedule, decide on dates and times. Record your plan on a calendar. Make sure that group members understand the meeting commitments they are making.

Designate Tasks

Will you need to make arrangements for speakers? Will you need to gather materials such as books, DVDs, or other resources? Will you need to make arrangements for a retreat or a field trip? Who will do such tasks? Who will be willing to serve on a worship and celebration team for the final meeting together? Make these decisions as a group and record them. Again, make sure that group members understand the commitments they are making.

Pray and Practice (5 minutes)

Practice for the "Go and Do" Portion of the Study

Thank the group for what they have contributed to the planning process for the weeks ahead. Encourage group members to do the following:

- Contact their faithful friend each week for coffee, lunch, a walk, or a phone conversation during the "Go and Do" portion of the study.
- Talk together about the plans the group has made and about the various activities they will experience as a group.
- Continue to use the questions in the faithful friends material in Session 1 of their study & reflection guide, "An Introduction to This Study Series" (pages 13–14), to stimulate their conversations.

Closing Prayer

Share prayer concerns. Invite participants to pray for their faithful friend and for the group this week and to pray for the meetings in the "Go and Do" portion of the study.

Close with a prayer asking God to support the group's plan for practicing attentiveness in the weeks ahead. Pray that each participant will sense God's support and the encouragement of the group.

Additional Helps

IDEAS FOR "GO AND DO"

The idea prompts provided in the study & reflection guide for use in Session 6, "Planning the Next Steps Together" (pages 60–61), should generate many possibilities for what you might "go and do" together. If your group needs help responding to these idea prompts, you can suggest the following:

Lectio Divina Scripture Passages

Plan one or more sessions in which you will explore what Jesus teaches about prayer in Scriptures such as Matthew 6:1-13.

Behavioral Changes to Make

Plan a group session that focuses on the everyday skill of listening. You can ask a pastor or counselor for resources related to active listening skills.

Ministry Events to Consider

Use a session to plan and implement a prayer ministry in your church. You can have your group pray for every person in your church throughout the "Go and Do" portion of the study and beyond. Send church members a friendly card letting them know the date that your group will be praying for them.

Mission Work to Conceive and Implement

Talk with your mission committee about possibilities for mission trips in the U.S. or abroad in which you can offer both prayer and action. Organize your trip to be an expression of prayer. Precede the trip with learning about the mission and praying for it, then take the trip and follow up with reflection on the experience.

Speakers to Invite

Invite someone from another church or religious background to come and share her or his perspectives on prayer. You might invite someone from a convent or monastery or perhaps someone from the Jewish or Islam faith to speak to your group about prayer in their tradition.

Field Trips, Retreats, Pilgrimages to Take

Many monasteries offer their facilities to visitors who want to take time apart for prayer. Plan a visit or retreat at a monastery.

Books to Read, Movies to See

Read one of the following books. Discuss how the book relates to the Christian trait of attentiveness.

- *Keeping the Sabbath Wholly: Ceasing, Resting, Embracing, Feasting,* by Marva J. Dawn (Wm. B. Eerdmans Publishing Company, 1989).
- *Lost in Wonder: Rediscovering the Spiritual Art of Attentiveness,* by Esther de Waal (Liturgical Press, 2003).
- *Receiving the Day: Christian Practices for Opening the Gift of Time,* by Dorthy C. Bass (Jossey-Bass, 2000).

Watch the movie *Radio* (2003), starring Ed Harris and Cuba Gooding Jr. Talk about how the movie illustrates attentiveness as a practice. How do the characters either listen or not listen?

Other Ideas

Every aspect of life offers opportunities to practice attentiveness together. Plan a trip to a shopping mall. Observe the people there. Think about what the scene suggests regarding life in our culture. What difference might the practice of attentiveness make in such a setting?

A SAMPLE PLAN

Your group might plan a series of weekly meetings in which members would explore and practice a variety of ways to pray. They could choose a book such as *50 Ways to Pray: Practices From Many Traditions and Times,* by Teresa A. Blythe (Abingdon Press, 2006) or *Prayer: Finding the Heart's True Home,* by Richard J. Foster (HarperSanFrancisco, 1992). If you choose this book study option, you might plan a series of sessions structured like Sessions 2–5 in the "Come and See" portion of the study, using some or all of the following steps.

Welcome—Greet group members as they arrive.
Psalm and Silence—Choose the psalms you would like to pray.
Look and Listen—Read portions of the study book you choose.
Reflect and Respond—Discuss what you have read, and have the
    group try a prayer practice that you have explored.
Lectio Divina—Select Scriptures on the subject of prayer.
Pray and Practice—Make assignments for the next session and pray
    a closing prayer.

Encourage faithful friends to continue to contact one another
and to talk about what the group has experienced together.

IDEAS FOR WORSHIP AND CELEBRATION

The final session of the study is a worship and celebration.
The group who volunteered during Session 6, "Planning the Next
Steps Together," will plan and implement this worship and celebration. Beginning with a meal is a good way to enjoy the friendships
developed during this study of the Christian practice of attentiveness. Below are some suggestions to stimulate ideas. You may want
to continue such practices as praying a psalm and lectio divina.
You also may want to invite your pastor to serve Holy Communion
during this worship and celebration. Be sure to make such
arrangements ahead of time.

• Create a worship center.
• Share a meal.
• Pray a psalm.
• Sing hymns and praise choruses.
• Read the Bible.
• Share testimonies or faith stories.
• Make a commitment to God.
• Celebrate Holy Communion or a love feast.
• Create a litany prayer of thanksgiving.